CHANGE AND GROW

PUPPY TO DOG

Acknowledgements: Cover: getty images/Gary Randall, gettyimages/Dorling Kindersley, gettyimages/Dorling Kindersley, gettyimages/Martin Harvey. p1 gettyimages/Steve Shott, p2 gettyimages/Dorling Kindersley, p3 getty images/Photodisc, p5 gettyimages/Tracy Morgan, pp6–7 gettyimages/Jane Burton, p8 gettyimages/Time & Life Pictures, p9 gettyimages/Dorling Kindersley, p10 gettyimages/Dorling Kindersley, p11 gettyimages/Dorling Kindersley, p12 gettyimages/Jane Burton, p13 gettyimages/Jane Burton, gettyimages/Tracy Morgan, p14 gettyimages/Steve Shott, p15 gettyimages/Steve Shott, p16 gettyimages/GK Hart/Vikki Hart, gettyimages/Martin Harvey, p17 gettyimages/Photodisc, p18 gettyimages/Tracy Morgan, gettyimages/Steve Lyne, p19 gettyimages/Stockbyte, p20 gettyimages/Gandee Vasan, p21 gettyimages/Dorling Kindersley, gettyimages/Steve Lyne, p22 gettyimages/GK Hart/Vikki Hart, p23 gettyimages/Dorling Kindersley, gettyimages/Gk Hart/vikki Hart, p24 gettyimages/Steve Shott.

This edition is published by Scholastic Inc.,
557 Broadway, New York, NY 10012, by arrangement with Parragon.

Distributed by:
Scholastic Australia Pty. Ltd, Gosford NSW
Scholastic Canada Ltd., Markham, Ontario
Scholastic New Zealand Ltd., Greenmount, Auckland

Scholastic and associated logos are trademarks and/or registered trademarks of Scholastic Inc.

Parragon
Queen Street House
4 Queen Street
Bath BA1 1HE, UK

Copyright © Parragon Books Ltd 2009

©2009 Discovery Communications, LLC. Discovery Kids, DiscoveryFacts and related logos and indicia are trademarks of Discovery Communications, LLC, used under license. All rights reserved. *discoverykids.com*

ISBN 978-1-4454-1081-4

10 9 8 7 6 5 4 3 2 1

Printed in Guangzhou, China

CHANGE AND GROW

PUPPY TO DOG

LIVE. LEARN. DISCOVER.

Steve Parker

PARRAGON

Bath · New York · Singapore · Hong Kong · Cologne · Delhi
Melbourne · Amsterdam · Johannesburg · Auckland · Shenzhen

A NEW LIFE BEGINS

A newborn puppy is small and helpless. The day after it's born, you may think it is just a day old. But the puppy has already been growing inside its mother's body for nine weeks.

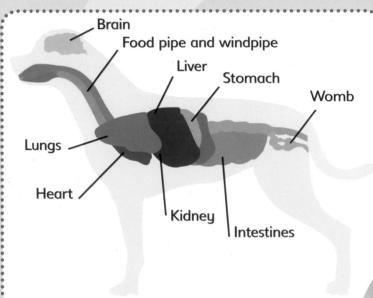

Brain

Food pipe and windpipe

Liver

Stomach

Womb

Lungs

Heart

Kidney

Intestines

Puppy's parents

The male and female dogs get together and mate. This makes the puppy start to grow.

Dad's coat is brown.

A safe place

The puppy grows inside a baglike part of the body called the womb. It gets food from its mother through a special tube called the cord.

Our puppies will be beautiful!

A puppy grows inside its mother for nine weeks—a baby elephant grows inside its mother for two years!

DiscoveryFact™

Look alike

Some of the puppies will look like Dad. Some will look like Mom. Some might look like a cross between the two.

Mom's ears are longer.

LIFE BEFORE BIRTH

When a female dog is carrying puppies, she is pregnant. She will probably have between four and six puppies growing and changing inside her.

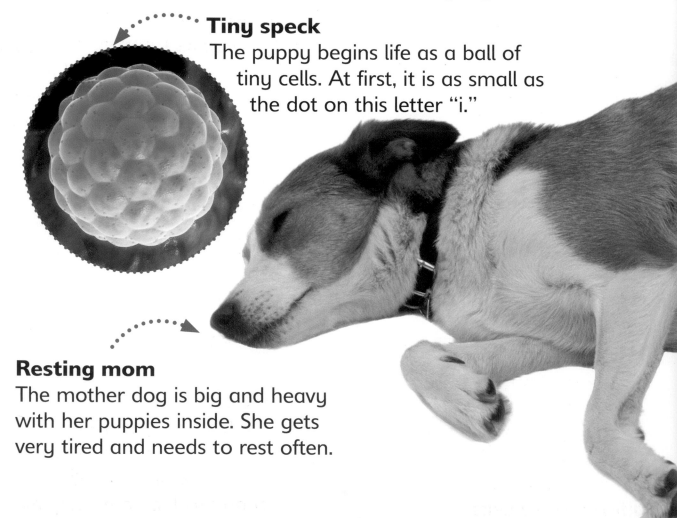

Tiny speck
The puppy begins life as a ball of tiny cells. At first, it is as small as the dot on this letter "i."

Resting mom
The mother dog is big and heavy with her puppies inside. She gets very tired and needs to rest often.

Taking shape

Safe inside its mother, the puppy's ears, eyes, nose, and mouth slowly develop. After a few weeks, it also has tiny paws and a very short tail.

Getting ready

Soon the puppy will start to grow some fur. It will be ready to enter the outside world in a few more weeks.

Ready to feed

The nipples on her belly swell with milk, ready to feed her puppies.

HERE I COME!

Puppies are usually born at night. The mother dog lies down quietly—and in the morning the puppies are there! She looks after each one carefully.

Somewhere safe

The mother chooses a safe, quiet place to have her puppies. She may get worried if there are other animals or people around.

Licked clean

The puppies are born one by one. The mother gently licks them clean and keeps them warm.

The new litter

It can take more than six hours for all the puppies to be born. The group of puppies is called a litter.

The largest recorded litter was 20 puppies—that's a lot of work for just one mother dog!

DiscoveryFact™

EAT, SLEEP, EAT, SLEEP

A new puppy is chubby and floppy, with short fur. Its eyes are shut, it cannot hear very well, and it has no teeth. But it has a good sense of smell!

First food

The puppies use their sense of smell to find milk. They wiggle up to a nipple, latch on, and take their first drink.

Each puppy has its own nipple.

Pushy pups

Sometimes the puppies push each other out of the way.

Hungry pups

A good feeding can take half an hour. The puppies press their paws against their mother's belly to help the milk flow.

Sleepyheads

Newborn puppies snuggle up with their brothers and sisters to keep warm. When they are not eating, they sleep.

LEARNING FAST

A young puppy grows fast as it feeds on its mother's milk. After just one week, a puppy is twice as big as it was when it was born!

At first, the puppy cannot see well.

Eyes open
At two weeks, the puppy's eyes open. It can look around and see its family for the first time.

Wobbly walk

At three weeks old, the puppy can hear well. It tries to walk, but at first it wobbles a lot and falls over.

Food for thought

Then the puppy's teeth start to grow. It still drinks its mother's milk, but will also nibble solid puppy food from a bowl.

Fun and Games

As the puppy grows bigger and stronger, it makes more noise and moves around more. By the time it is two months old, it no longer needs its mother's milk.

Play time

Every day, the puppy can run faster and jump higher. It plays games like "chase," "tug-of-war," and "play-fight" with its sisters and brothers.

Chew, chew

Puppies like to bite and chew things. This is how they learn about the world, and about what is good to eat and what is not.

A puppy has sharp teeth.

Leaving home

After two months, the puppy is ready to leave its mother, brothers, and sisters. It is time to start life with a new family.

Pet dogs are related to wild wolves, which were first tamed by people more than 12,000 years ago.

DiscoveryFact™

A NEW HOME

When a puppy first arrives at its new family home, it may whine and cry for its mother. It will settle down when it realizes its new home is a safe, happy place.

A place to sleep

The puppy needs a place of its own, where it can rest and sleep. A basket or box is perfect.

Play with me!

The puppy loves to play. It will chase toys and try to catch them. In the wild this would be good practice for hunting, but it is also great exercise.

That's my name
The puppy listens to its owners when they speak. If they say its name clearly and often, the puppy will soon learn what it is called.

The American coyote, the African wild dog, and the Australian dingo are three types of wild dog.

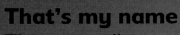

DiscoveryFact™

Hello, Max!

Good boy, Max!

GROWING UP FAST

By about four months old, the puppy is slimmer and stronger. It can run fast and jump high. It starts to get its grown-up teeth—and tests them by chewing even more!

Something to chew

The puppy chews for comfort when its new teeth are coming through. It needs its own toys to stop it from chewing things it shouldn't.

House training

At first, the puppy cannot control when it goes to the bathroom. It needs to learn to use an old newspaper. After a few months it should be "house-trained"—it can wait until it goes outside.

Learning words
The puppy should slowly
learn that it is part of
a family—but not the
boss. Its owners
help it learn simple
commands like "Sit!"
"Stay!" and "Come!"

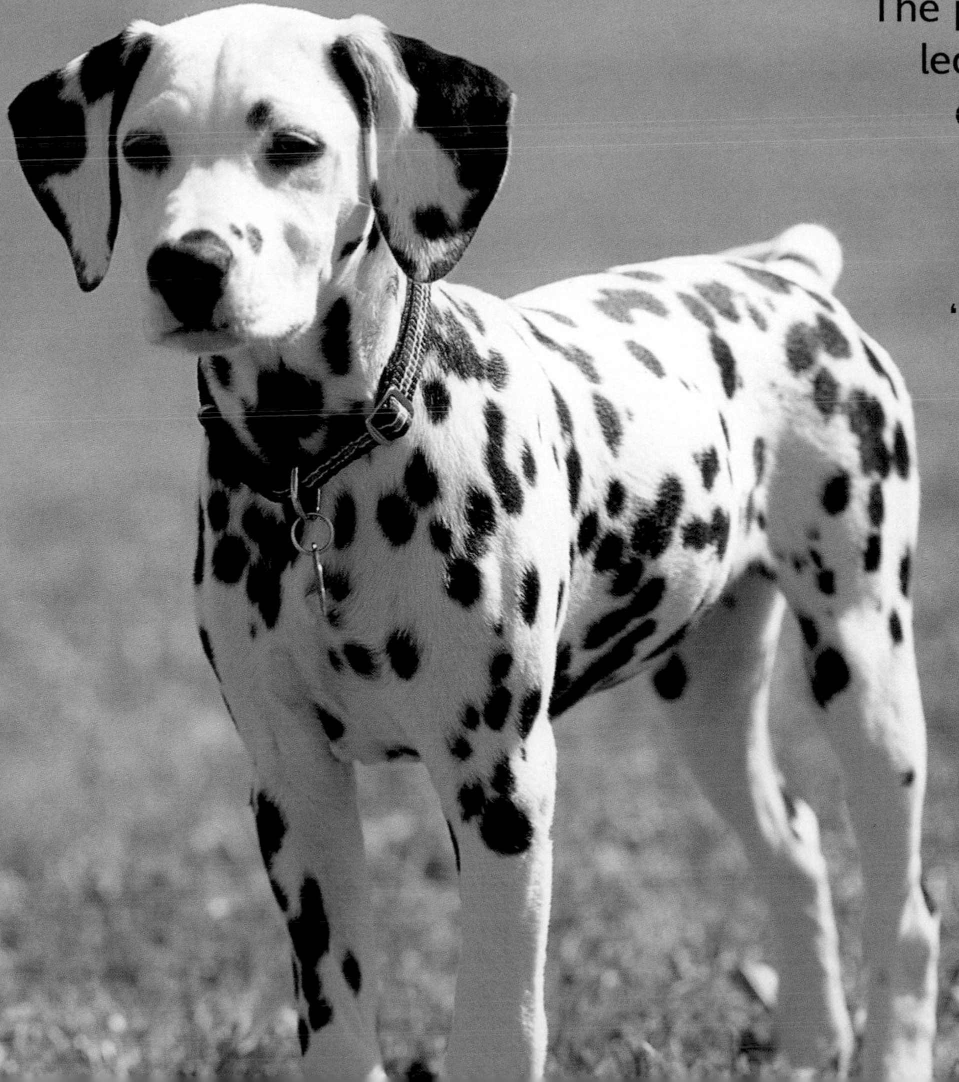

Come!

Best Behavior

Young dogs need a lot of walks and exercise. They like to play with other dogs, but they need to learn not to get too excited so they don't bite or fight.

Collar and leash
The puppy needs to get used to wearing a collar and leash. It should be taught not to pull on the leash and to "heel."

Heel boy!
A dog that pulls hard on its leash can hurt its neck and have breathing problems.

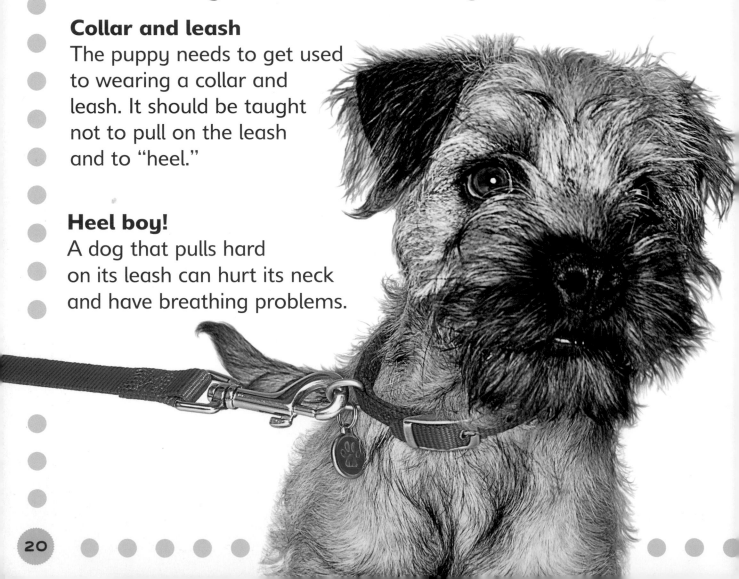

A bark can be a warning.

Hush puppy

A young dog who gets into the habit of barking too much can become a problem. Its owners should teach it to stay quiet most of the time.

Being brushed

A dog keeps clean by licking its fur. Its owner should also groom it every day. This reminds the dog that it is part of a family, and that its owner is the boss!

ALL GROWN UP

By the time it is about one year old, the puppy is grown up and can have puppies of its own. Even though it has finished growing, it can still learn new things.

Help from the vet

Like people, dogs sometimes get sick or hurt. An animal doctor called a vet can help them get better.

There are over 400 breeds of dog— from tiny Chihuahuas to massive Great Danes.

DiscoveryFact™

Growing old

By about 10 years of age, some breeds of dogs are starting to get old. But others can live well past 20—and one reached 29!

Dog breeds

These are just a few of the many different breeds of dog.

Golden Retriever

Dalmatian

Alsatian

Spaniel

Bulldog

Westhighland Terrier

LIFE CYCLE

Mating
The male and female dogs mate. The puppy grows inside its mother for 9 weeks.

Birth
The puppy is born and starts drinking its mother's milk.

1 year
The puppy is now an adult dog. It can have puppies of its own.

32–40 weeks
The puppy is now almost full-grown.

1 to 2 weeks
The puppy's eyes open.

24–32 weeks
The puppy needs 2 meals a day, and lots of exercise and training.

2–3 weeks
The puppy's ears are now working properly.

16–24 weeks
The puppy chews a lot. Its muscles become much stronger.

3–6 weeks
The puppy's baby teeth grow. It starts to bark and wag its tail.

12–16 weeks
The puppy's adult teeth grow. It may try to become the family boss.

7–12 weeks
The puppy learns its name. It still needs 4 meals every day.

5–7 weeks
The puppy stops drinking its mother's milk and starts solid food.

KITTEN TO CAT

CHANGE AND GROW

Acknowledgements: Cover: getty images/Patricia Doyle, getty images/Marc Henrie, gettyimages/Dorling Kindersley, gettyimages/Vincenzo Lombardo, gettyimages/Marc Henrie. p1 gettyimages/Jane Burton, p2 gettyimages/Dorling Kindersley, p3 gettyimages/Peety Cooper, p4 gettyimages/Jane Burton, p5 gettyimages/3D4Medical.com, pp6–7 gettyimages/Jane Burton, p8 gettyimages/Michael Blann, p9 gettyimages/Steve Gorton and Tim Ridley, gettyimages/Jane Burton, p10 gettyimages/Jane Burton, p11 gettyimages/Steve Shott, p12 gettyimages/ Vincenzo Lombardo, p13 gettyimages/Dorling Kindersley, p14 getty/images/GK Hart/Vikki Hart, p15 gettyimages/Dorling Kindersley, gettyimages/Jane Burton, p16 gettyimages/Koki Iino, gettyimages/TSI Pictures, p17 gettyimages/Jane Burton, p18 gettyimages/Jane Burton, p19 gettyimages/Martin Ruegner, p20 gettyimages/Steve Gorton and Tim Ridley, gettyimages/Ove Eriksson, p21 gettyimages/Sharon Dominick, p22 gettyimages/Stockbyte, p23 gettyimages/Kevin Fitzgerald, p24 gettyimages/Peety Cooper.

Discovery Kids

Change and Grow

Kitten to Cat

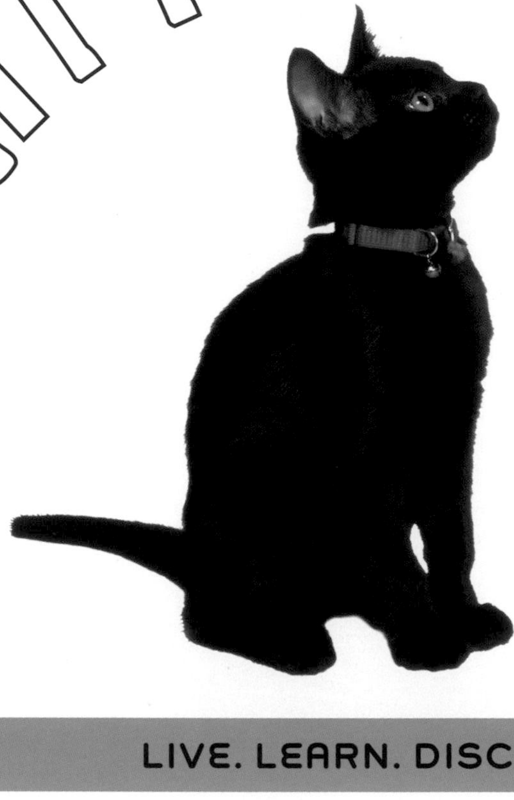

LIVE. LEARN. DISCOVER.

Steve Parker

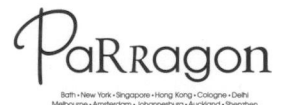

Parragon
Bath • New York • Singapore • Hong Kong • Cologne • Delhi
Melbourne • Amsterdam • Johannesburg • Auckland • Shenzhen

LIFE BEGINS

The female cat had her first kittens last summer. Now it's spring and she is ready to have some more.

Getting together

At first, the female cat does not like the male cat—in fact she spits at him! But after a while they get together and mate.

The male and female cat may not look alike.

A mother cat is called a queen, but a father cat is not called a king— he is known as a tom.

DiscoveryFact™

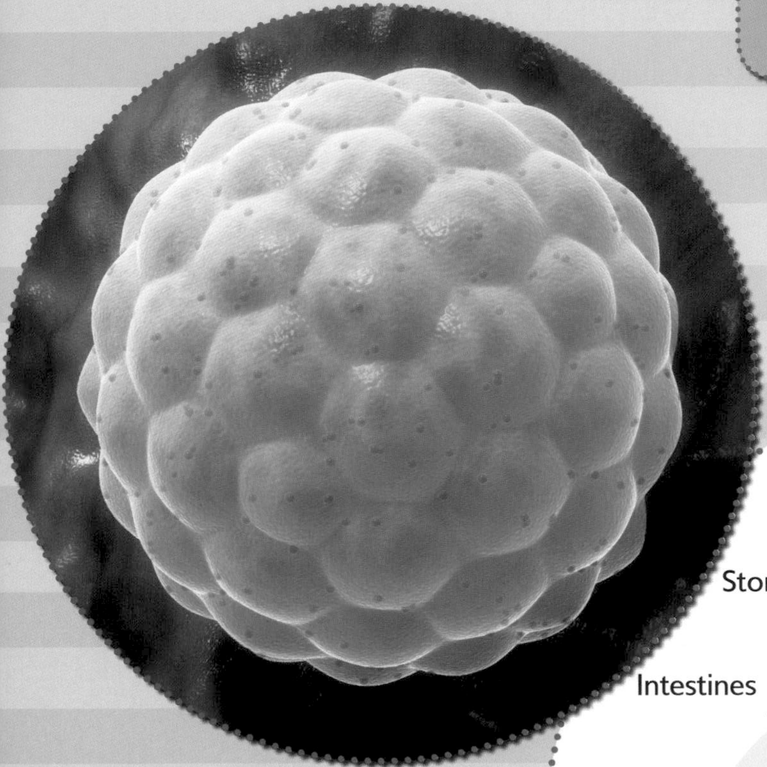

The very beginning
The new kittens begin life as tiny dots, as small as the one on this letter "i."

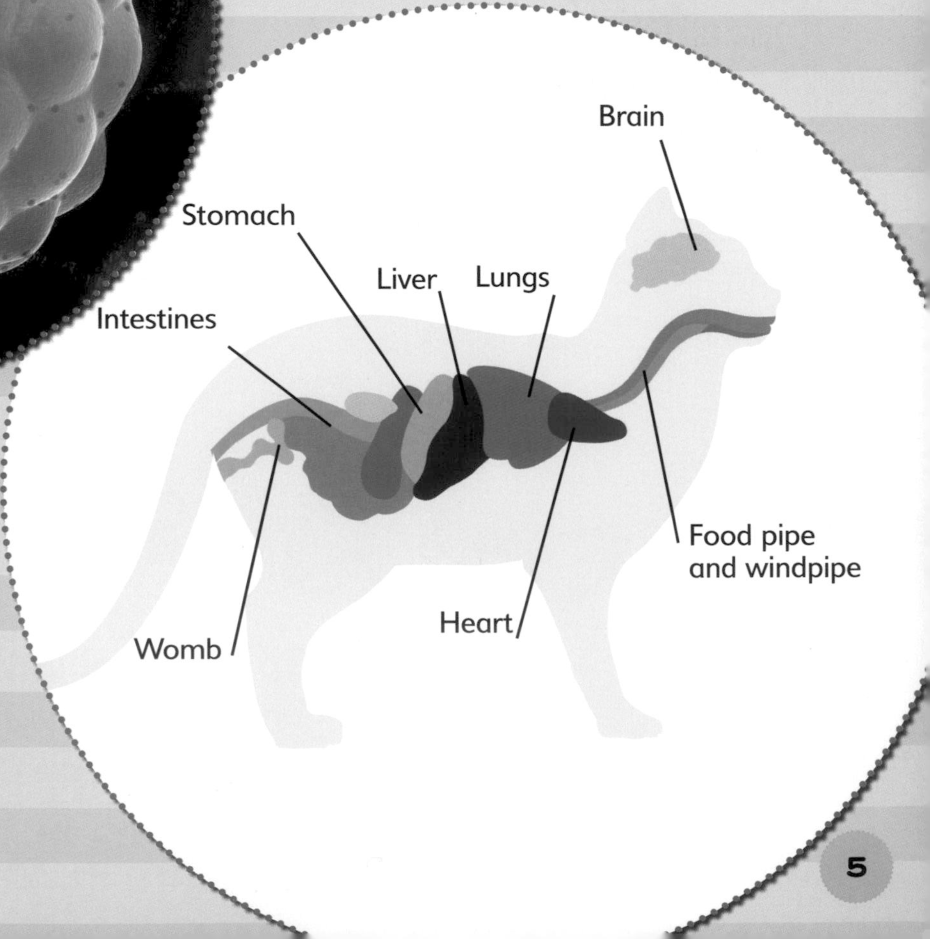

Brain
Stomach
Liver
Lungs
Intestines
Food pipe and windpipe
Heart
Womb

Safe inside
The kittens grow inside the mother's body, in a baglike part of the body called the womb, or uterus.

GROWING INSIDE

The tiny kitten grows fast inside its mother's body. Soon its body parts start to form, and it begins to look more like a cat.

Special delivery
The kitten gets food from its mother's body along a ropelike part known as the cord.

Most mother cats have between 4 and 6 kittens at a time—the largest litter on record was 19 kittens!

DiscoveryFact™

Taking shape
The kitten's head and body grow. Then its eyes, legs, tail, and fur start to form.

HERE I AM!

The time is near for the mother cat to give birth. She is very heavy with the kittens inside her and needs to sleep and rest a lot.

Safe den
The mother cat looks for a quiet, dark place. She needs a safe den where she can give birth to her kittens. It might be a warm closet or an old cardboard box.

An average newborn kitten weighs three or four ounces—that's five times more than a house mouse.

DiscoveryFact™

One by one
The kittens come out one by one. Giving birth to them all takes the mother cat between one and ten hours.

Clean up
The group, or litter, of kittens are brothers and sisters. The mother cat licks them clean and keeps them warm.

WHAT CAN I DO?

The newborn kitten spends most of its time sleeping and eating. It stays close to its mother and snuggles up with its brothers and sisters to keep warm.

Feeding time
The kitten feeds on milk. It sucks the milk from a nipple on its mother's belly. Each kitten in a litter has its own nipple. It pushes with its front paws to help the milk flow.

Weak and helpless
When the kitten is born, its eyes are closed, it cannot hear, and it isn't strong enough to walk. Its mother moves it by gently picking it up with her mouth.

Newborn noises

Even a newborn kitten can make a noise. It squeaks to tell its mother when it is hungry.

Curious kitten

After about a week, the kitten's eyes start to open. It begins to stretch its legs and to crawl around.

Even an adult cat sleeps for around 18 hours a day—how lazy!

DiscoveryFact™

Squeak!

The kitten's eyes are open.

GROWING FAST

By three weeks old, the kitten is starting to walk and run. It's a little wobbly and gets tired quickly—often falling over or flopping down.

Look and listen
By four weeks the kitten can hear and see fairly well. It can see in the dark much better than we can. It also uses its long whiskers to feel its way around in the dark.

The kitten now has sharp teeth.

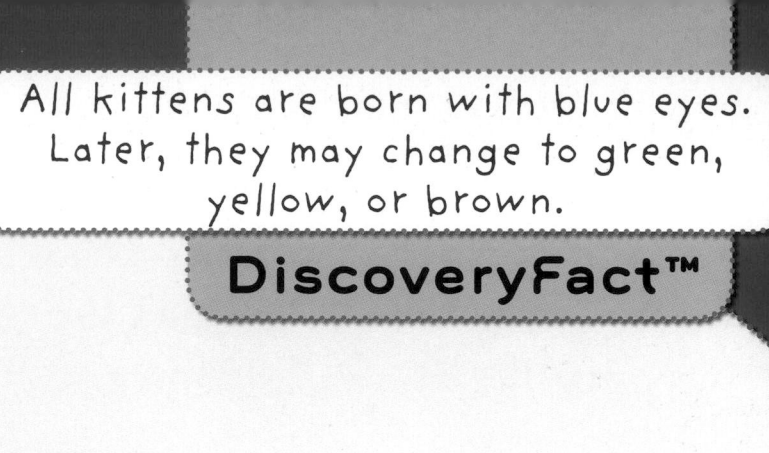

All kittens are born with blue eyes. Later, they may change to green, yellow, or brown.

DiscoveryFact™

Weaning

The kitten begins to explore away from its mother. Its teeth are growing. It starts to eat other foods and drinks less of its mother's milk. This time is known as weaning.

PLAYFUL PAWS

Cats are natural hunters—they love to chase and pounce. Kittens learn how to do this by playing.

Exercise is fun!
The kitten loves to explore and play with toys—and anything else it can get its paws on. It needs lots of exercise to make its muscles strong and improve its balance.

A kitten pats a toy.

Kittens love to climb—they sometimes climb too high, get stuck, and are too afraid to come back down!

DiscoveryFact™

Watching mom

The kittens learn from their mother. She plays with them and teaches them everything they need to know. They learn how to keep clean and where to go to the bathroom.

Boo!

Play fight!

The kittens creep up and pounce on anything that moves—often their brothers and sisters!

15

CAT CHAT

Most cats like some company. They love to be with people. If a kitten grows up with other animals—even dogs—they will probably be good friends.

"You're my friend!"
If a cat feels friendly, it rubs itself against its friends and "talks" by meowing.

Let's be friends!

Happy cat
A very happy cat purrs. It might even roll onto its back to have its tummy tickled.

Stay away
A scared or angry cat flattens its ears and hisses. It may also arch its back, fluff up its fur, and swish its tail.

Hiss!

Look out!
A cat who does not want to be touched may scratch or bite. So be careful!

17

TIME FOR A CHANGE

When the kitten is 9 to 12 weeks old it will be ready to leave its mother, brothers, and sisters. It's time for the kitten to meet its new family.

Settling in

The new owners must keep the kitten indoors for a few days. The kitten will need some time to settle in and learn where its food, water, and litter box are.

Busy, busy

The kitten needs a lot of attention and plenty of toys to play with.

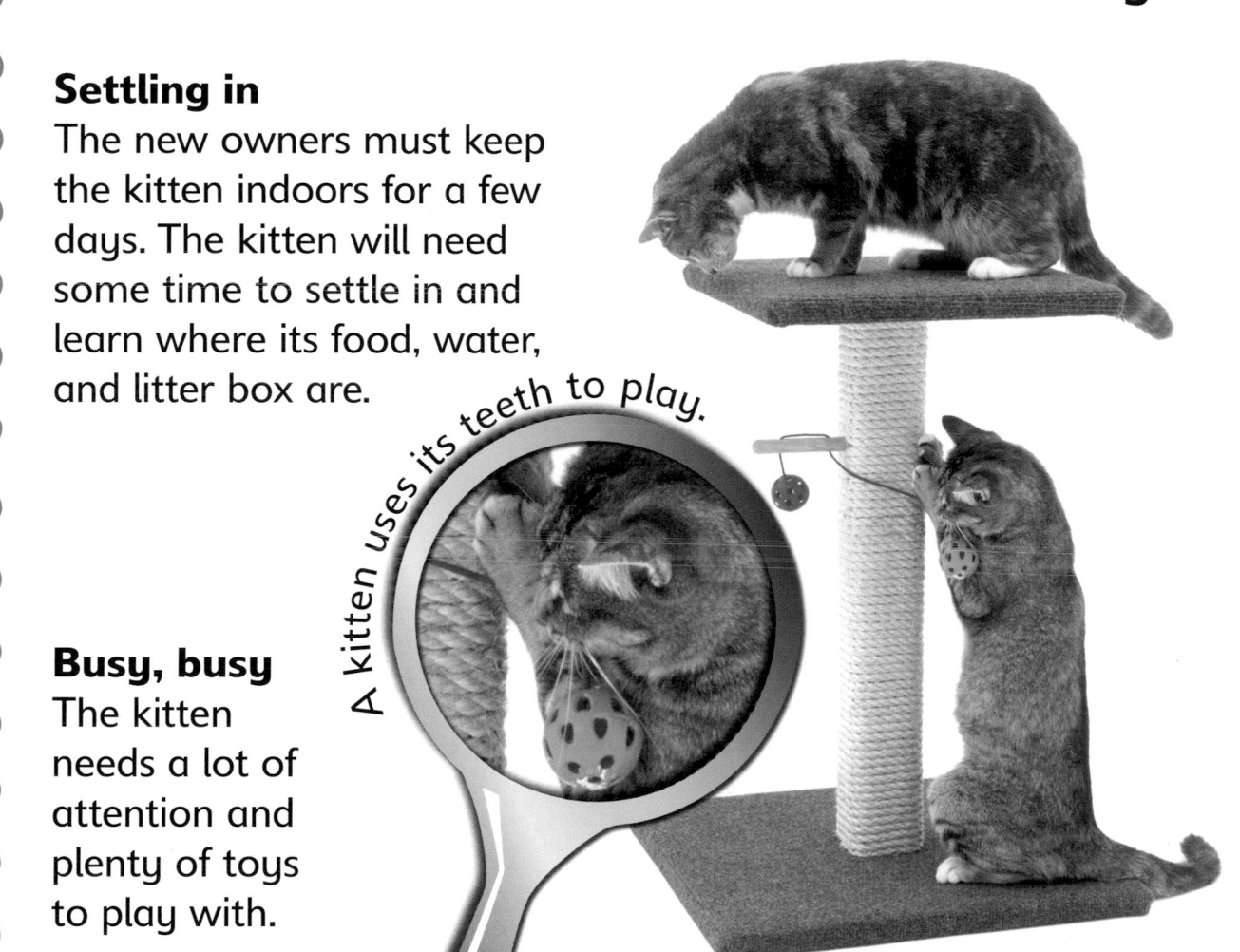

A kitten uses its teeth to play.

Out and about

Soon the kitten will be ready to go outside. It will love to play and explore, and it won't pay much attention to fences—jumping over them is good exercise!

ON MY OWN

When it is six months old, the cat is almost full-grown. It spends a lot of time outside hunting mice and birds, then comes inside to rest where it's warm.

Feeding time
An adult cat needs one or two meals a day of meat, fish, or canned or dried cat food.

Hunting fun
A well-fed cat hunts for fun, not because it is hungry!

Keeping clean
The cat cleans itself by licking its fur with its rough tongue. If it swallows too much fur it might cough up a slimy lump called a hair ball!

A cat's tongue is covered with little spikes called barbs, which help comb its fur. A lion's tongue is even rougher!

DiscoveryFact™

I'm busy!

ALL GROWN UP

By the time the cat is about one year old, she is an adult cat. She can now have kittens of her own.

Home sweet home

Most adult cats stay in the area around their home—this is their territory. Some toms wander much farther in search of queens to mate with.

Catnaps

A cat has favorite sleeping spots. The older it gets, the more it naps. It may nap for more than half the day.

LIFE CYCLE

Mating
The male and female mate. The kitten starts to grow inside its mother.

Birth
The kitten is born after nine weeks.

1 year
The kitten is now an adult cat. It can have kittens of its own.

First feelings
The kitten purrs, hisses, and squeaks to show its feelings.

6–8 months
The kitten is now almost full-grown.

1–2 weeks
The eyes and ears start to work, and the kitten starts to move around.

9–12 weeks
The kitten can now leave its mother and go to a new home.

2–3 weeks
The kitten's baby teeth start to grow.

9–12 weeks
Play becomes more serious; there may be fights with other cats.

3–4 weeks
The kitten walks and runs. It can use a litter box and clean itself.

8–9 weeks
All the kitten's baby teeth have grown. Its eyes are their adult color.

From 5 weeks
The kitten stops feeding on its mother's milk and eats solid food.